T0021150

Note: The 1001 little fish in this book are based on sardines.

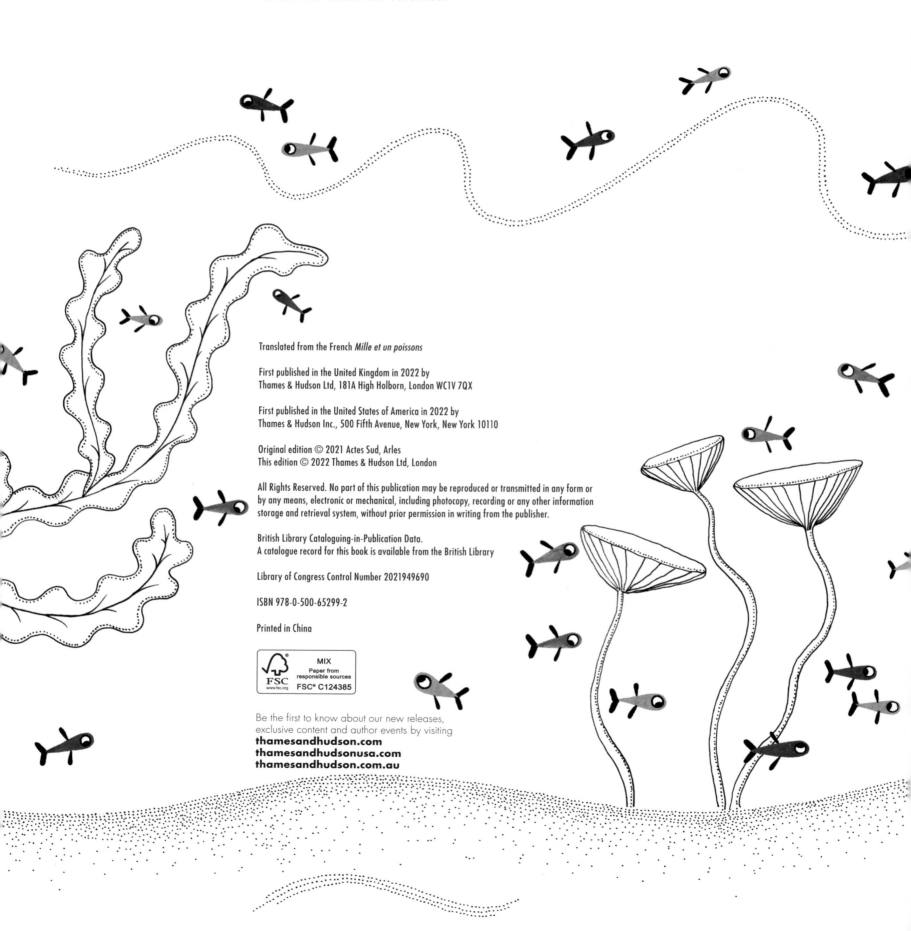

Translated from the French *Mille et un poissons*

First published in the United Kingdom in 2022 by
Thames & Hudson Ltd, 181A High Holborn, London WC1V 7QX

First published in the United States of America in 2022 by
Thames & Hudson Inc., 500 Fifth Avenue, New York, New York 10110

Original edition © 2021 Actes Sud, Arles
This edition © 2022 Thames & Hudson Ltd, London

All Rights Reserved. No part of this publication may be reproduced or transmitted in any form or by any means, electronic or mechanical, including photocopy, recording or any other information storage and retrieval system, without prior permission in writing from the publisher.

British Library Cataloguing-in-Publication Data.
A catalogue record for this book is available from the British Library

Library of Congress Control Number 2021949690

ISBN 978-0-500-65299-2

Printed in China

FSC
www.fsc.org

MIX
Paper from
responsible sources
FSC® C124385

Be the first to know about our new releases,
exclusive content and author events by visiting
thamesandhudson.com
thamesandhudsonusa.com
thamesandhudson.com.au

Joanna Rzezak

1001 FISH

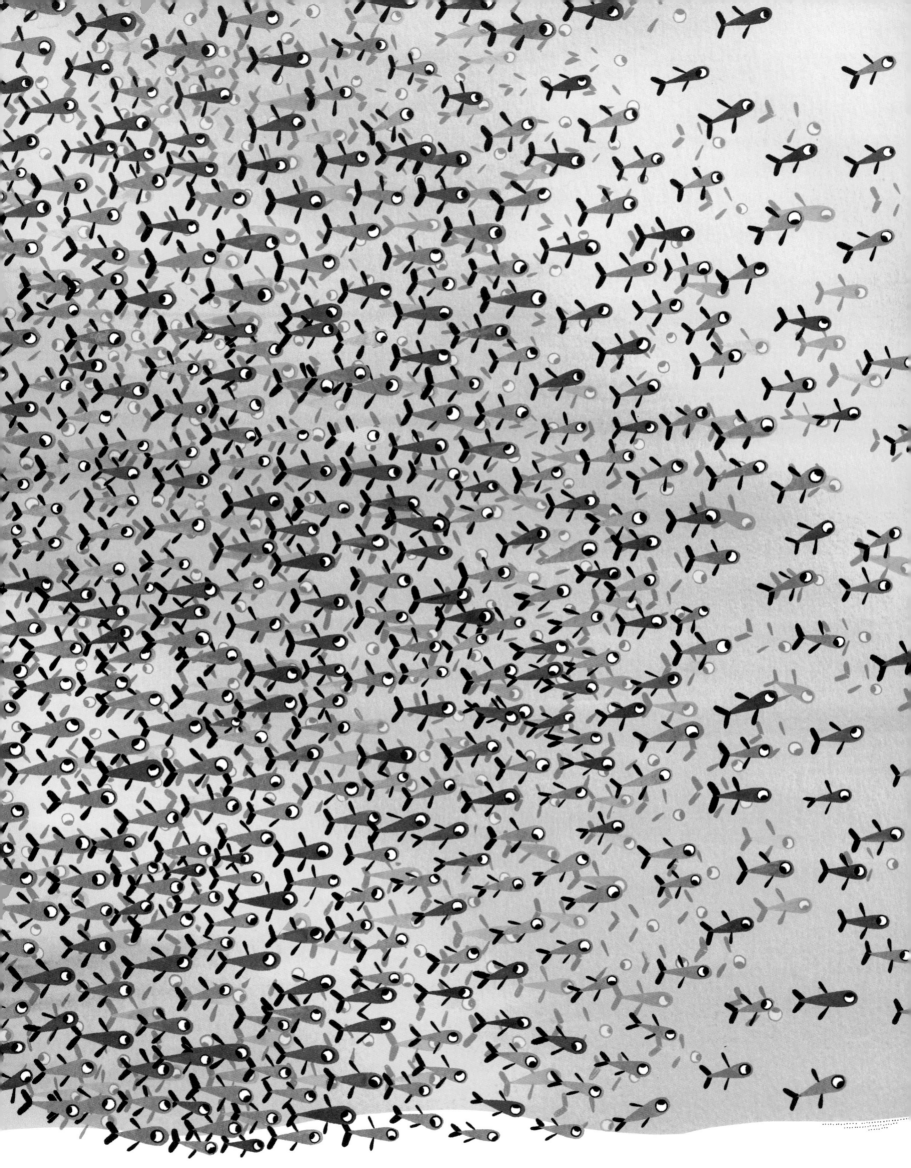

When the sun rises, the ocean comes to life. Now the night is over, these little fish feel safe. There's a wonderful world beneath the waves so they're off to explore! But they always stay close together, just in case.

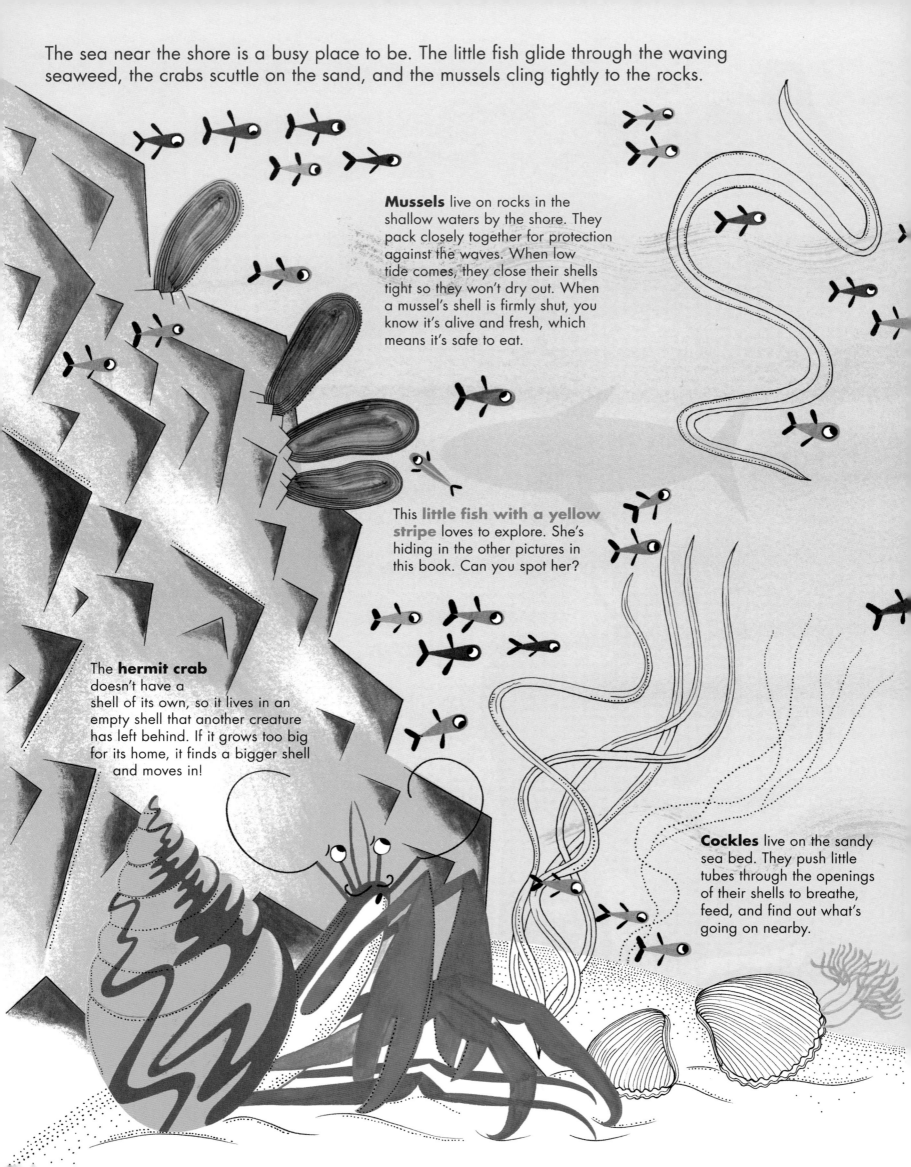

The sea near the shore is a busy place to be. The little fish glide through the waving seaweed, the crabs scuttle on the sand, and the mussels cling tightly to the rocks.

Mussels live on rocks in the shallow waters by the shore. They pack closely together for protection against the waves. When low tide comes, they close their shells tight so they won't dry out. When a mussel's shell is firmly shut, you know it's alive and fresh, which means it's safe to eat.

This **little fish with a yellow stripe** loves to explore. She's hiding in the other pictures in this book. Can you spot her?

The **hermit crab** doesn't have a shell of its own, so it lives in an empty shell that another creature has left behind. If it grows too big for its home, it finds a bigger shell and moves in!

Cockles live on the sandy sea bed. They push little tubes through the openings of their shells to breathe, feed, and find out what's going on nearby.

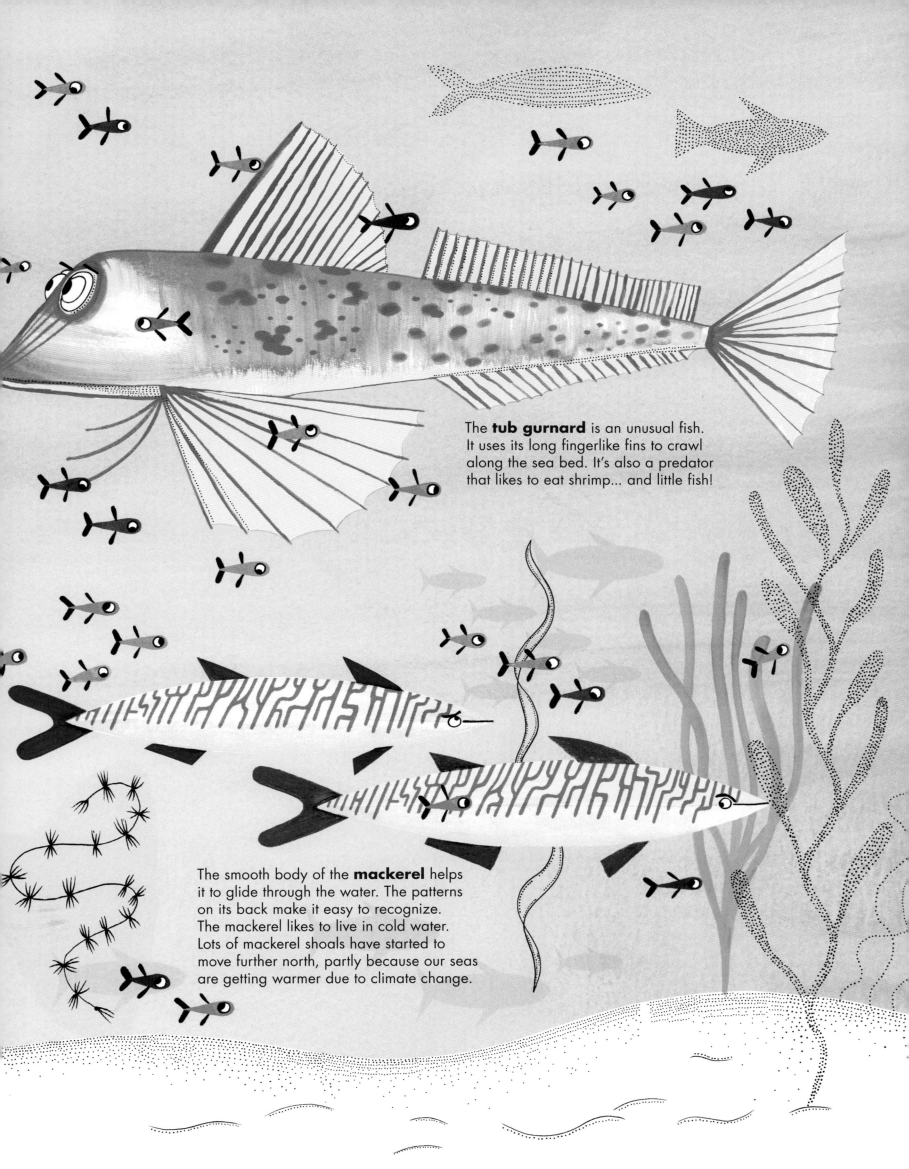

The **tub gurnard** is an unusual fish. It uses its long fingerlike fins to crawl along the sea bed. It's also a predator that likes to eat shrimp... and little fish!

The smooth body of the **mackerel** helps it to glide through the water. The patterns on its back make it easy to recognize. The mackerel likes to live in cold water. Lots of mackerel shoals have started to move further north, partly because our seas are getting warmer due to climate change.

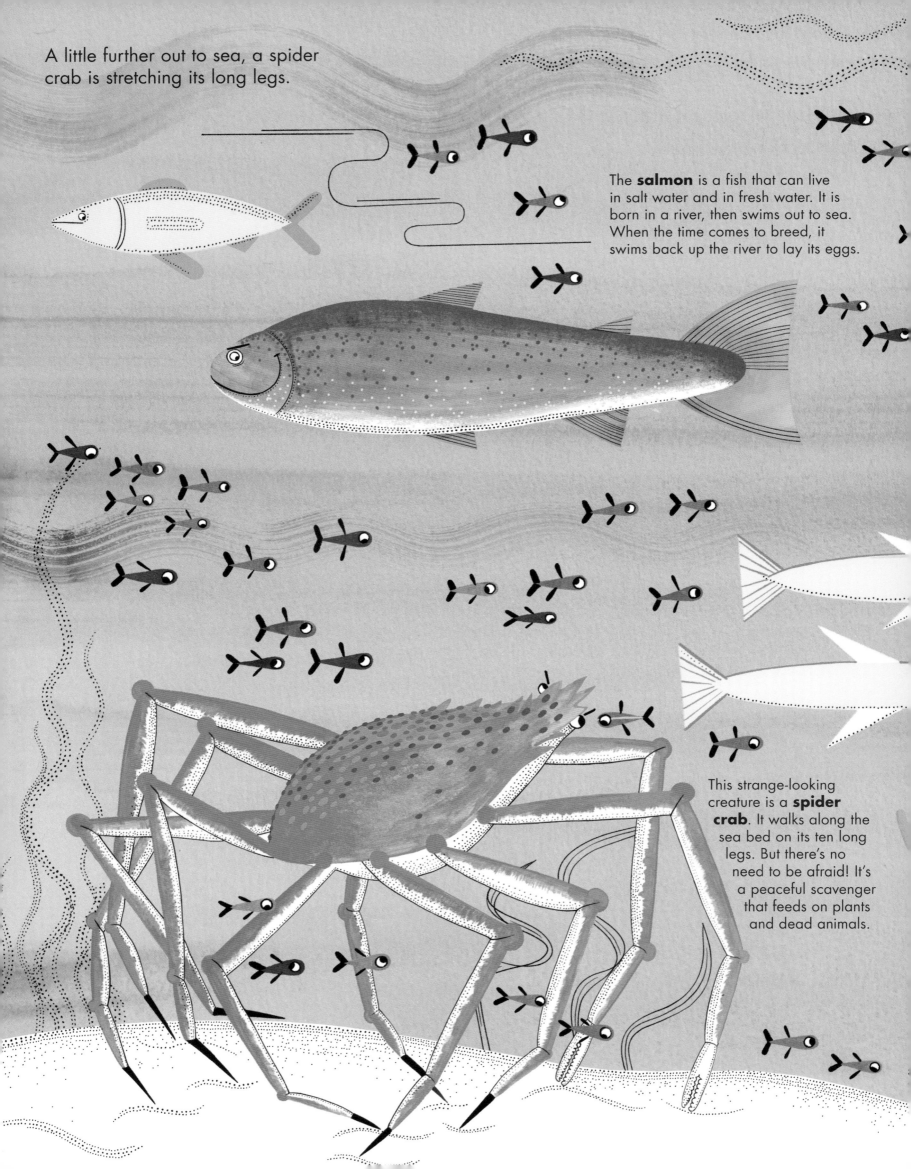

A little further out to sea, a spider crab is stretching its long legs.

The **salmon** is a fish that can live in salt water and in fresh water. It is born in a river, then swims out to sea. When the time comes to breed, it swims back up the river to lay its eggs.

This strange-looking creature is a **spider crab**. It walks along the sea bed on its ten long legs. But there's no need to be afraid! It's a peaceful scavenger that feeds on plants and dead animals.

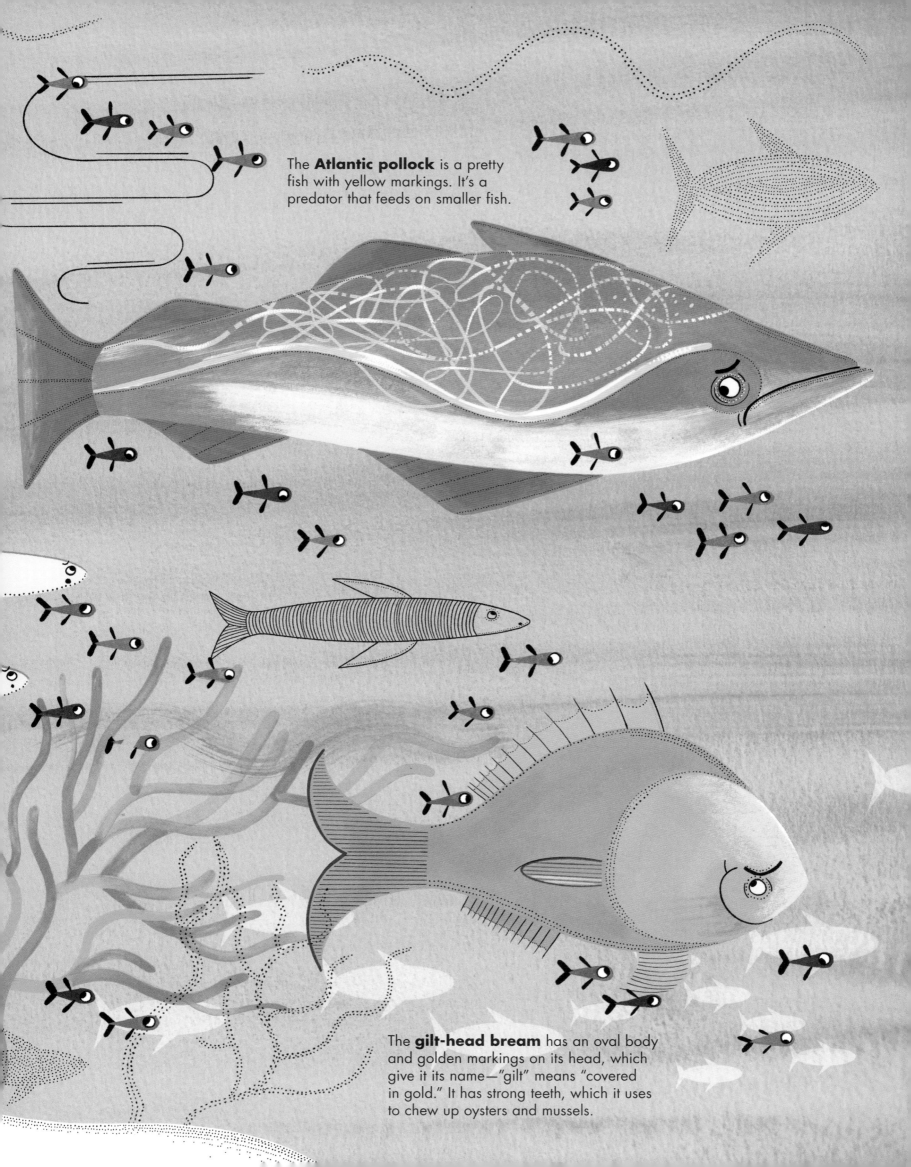

The **Atlantic pollock** is a pretty fish with yellow markings. It's a predator that feeds on smaller fish.

The **gilt-head bream** has an oval body and golden markings on its head, which give it its name—"gilt" means "covered in gold." It has strong teeth, which it uses to chew up oysters and mussels.

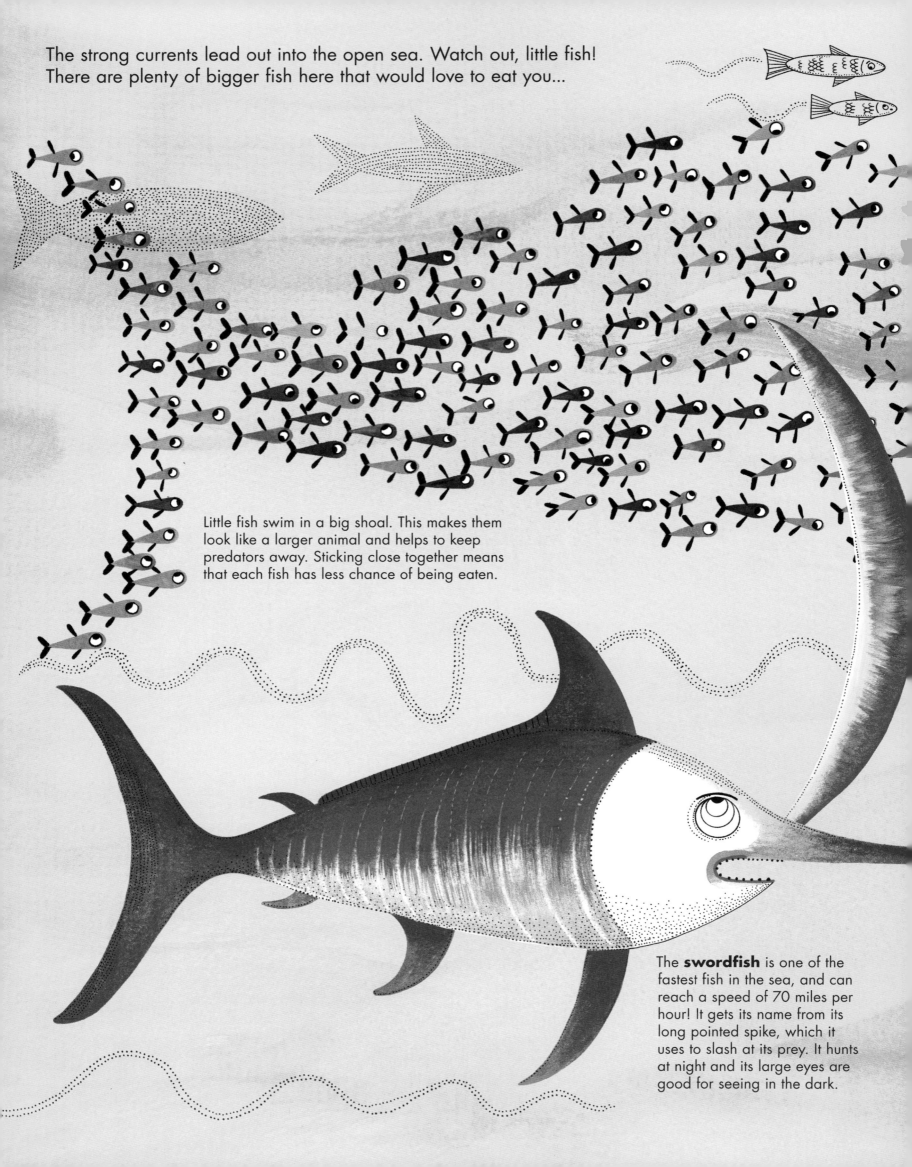

The strong currents lead out into the open sea. Watch out, little fish! There are plenty of bigger fish here that would love to eat you...

Little fish swim in a big shoal. This makes them look like a larger animal and helps to keep predators away. Sticking close together means that each fish has less chance of being eaten.

The **swordfish** is one of the fastest fish in the sea, and can reach a speed of 70 miles per hour! It gets its name from its long pointed spike, which it uses to slash at its prey. It hunts at night and its large eyes are good for seeing in the dark.

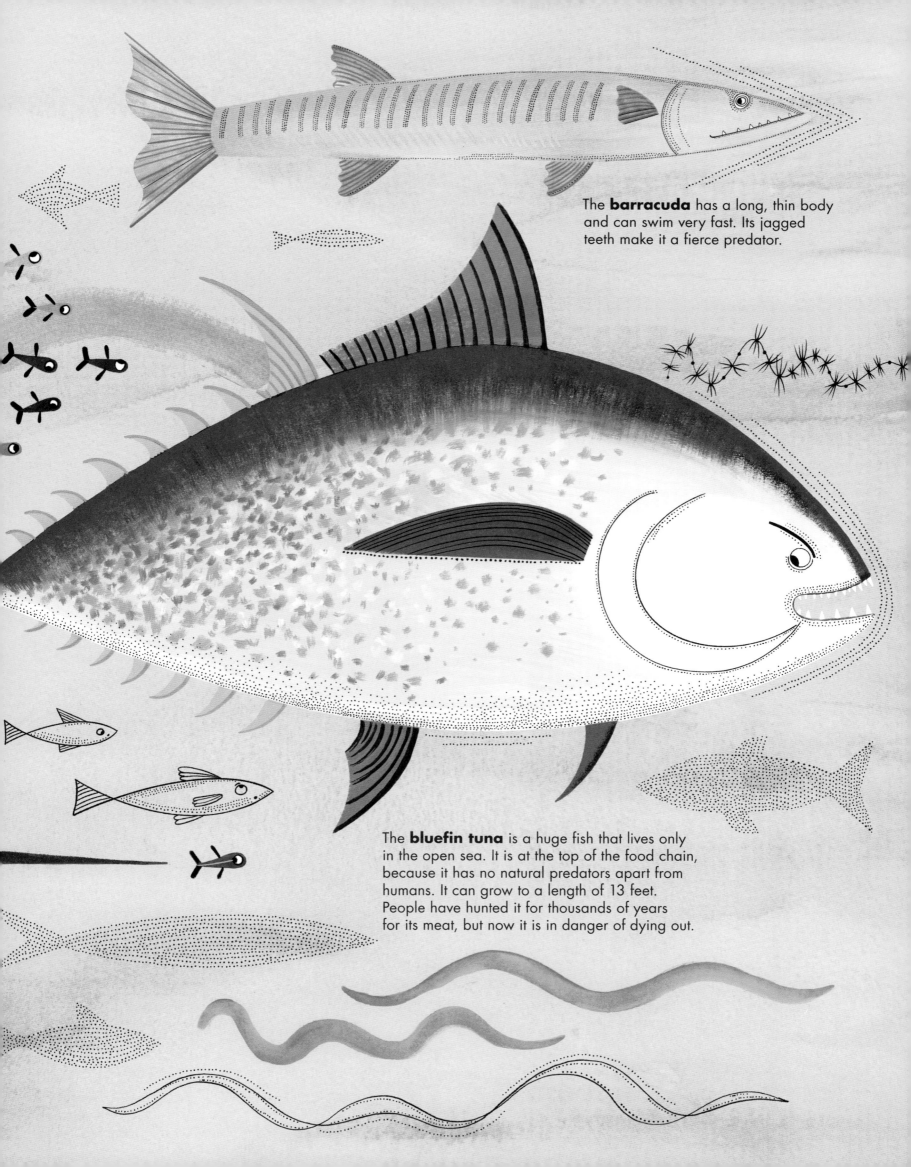

The **barracuda** has a long, thin body and can swim very fast. Its jagged teeth make it a fierce predator.

The **bluefin tuna** is a huge fish that lives only in the open sea. It is at the top of the food chain, because it has no natural predators apart from humans. It can grow to a length of 13 feet. People have hunted it for thousands of years for its meat, but now it is in danger of dying out.

Danger can come from the sky as well as the ocean! Seabirds love to eat fish and often dip their heads below the waves to snap up a tasty bite.

This big bird is a **great white pelican**. It is easy to recognize because of the huge stretchy pouch that hangs down below its beak. Using the pouch, it scoops up fish and swallows them whole. It can even scoop up several fish at once.

The **blue-footed booby** is an expert diver and can dive at 120 miles per hour! When hitting the water at high speed, it flattens its wings against its body and covers its eyes with special transparent eyelids. It can plunge as deep as 80 feet below the surface.

The **common tern** is a small seabird with a black cap of feathers on its head.

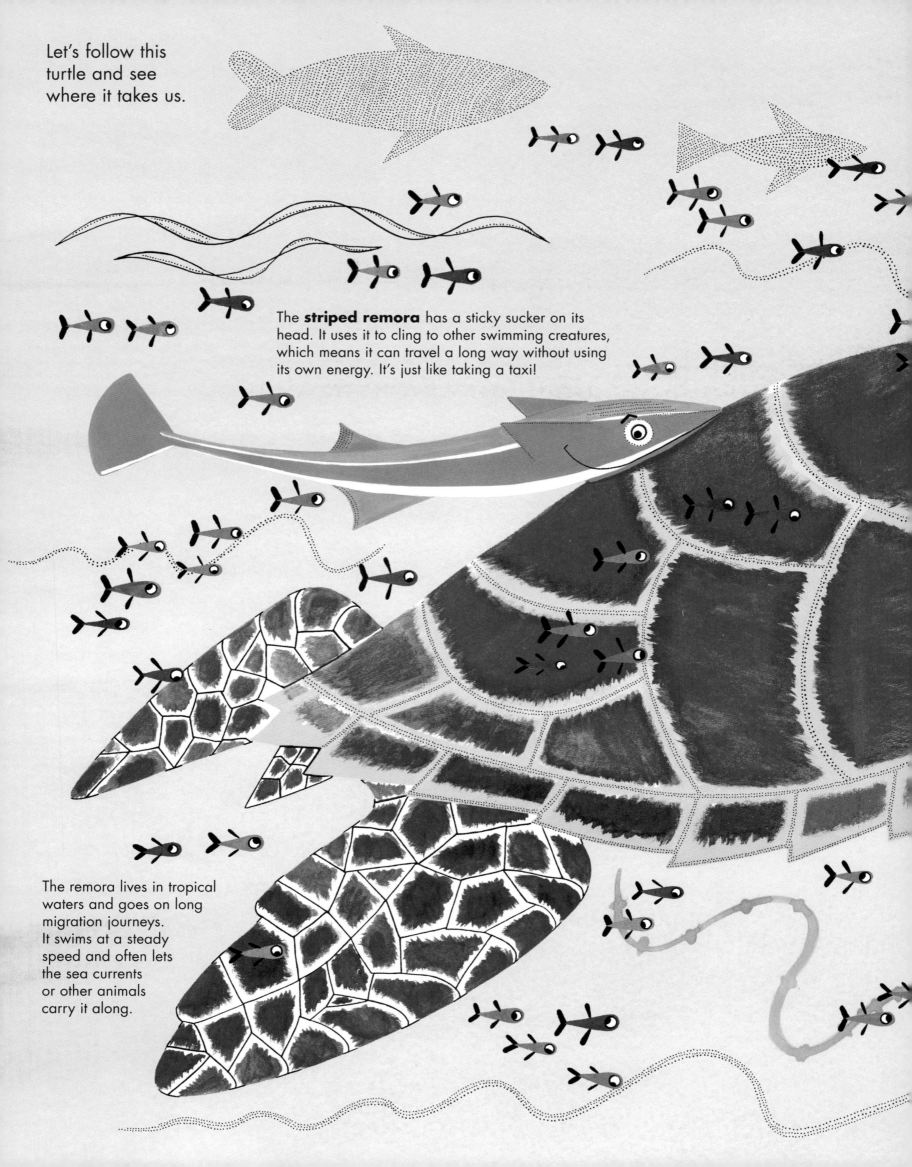

Let's follow this turtle and see where it takes us.

The **striped remora** has a sticky sucker on its head. It uses it to cling to other swimming creatures, which means it can travel a long way without using its own energy. It's just like taking a taxi!

The remora lives in tropical waters and goes on long migration journeys. It swims at a steady speed and often lets the sea currents or other animals carry it along.

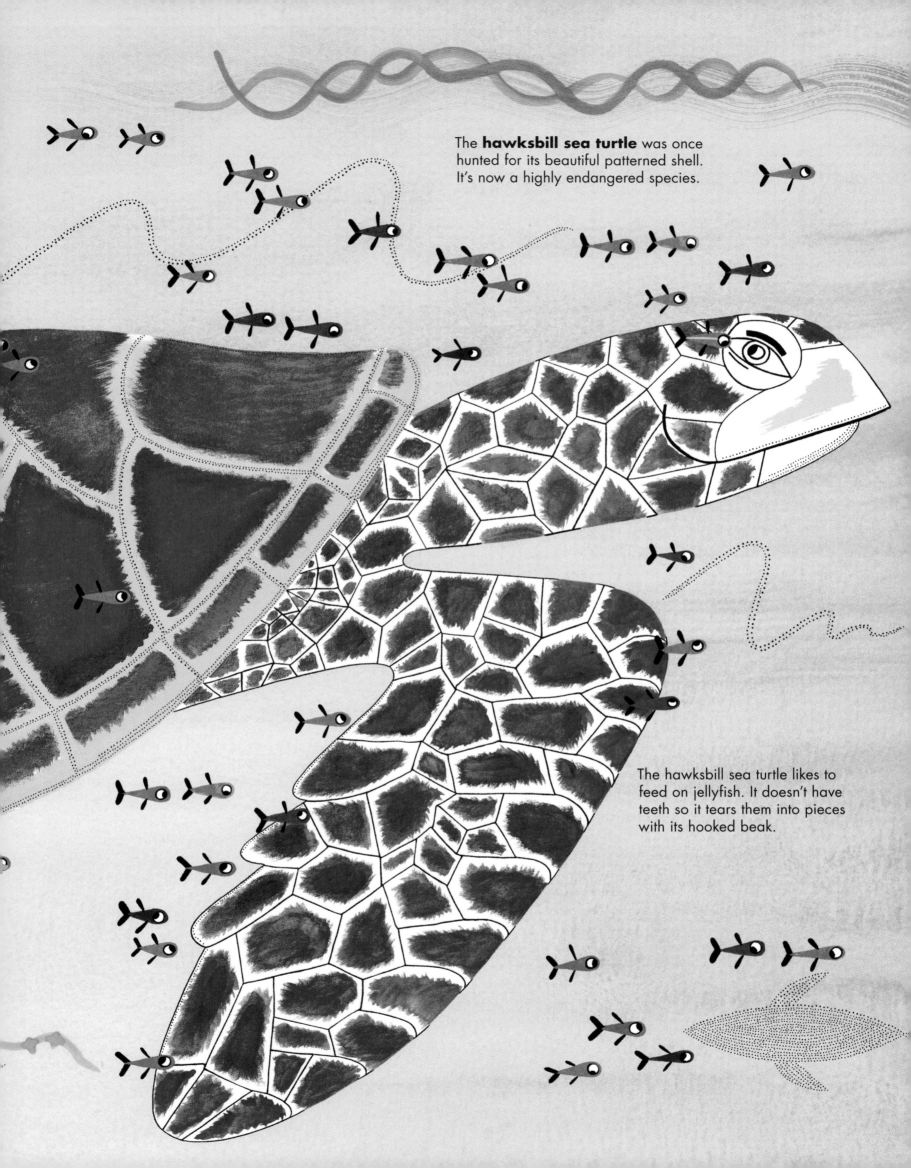

The **hawksbill sea turtle** was once hunted for its beautiful patterned shell. It's now a highly endangered species.

The hawksbill sea turtle likes to feed on jellyfish. It doesn't have teeth so it tears them into pieces with its hooked beak.

In the warm waters of the Caribbean, there's an amazing undersea world of colorful animals and plants.

Welcome to the coral reef! This is the home of lots of different fish, turtles and other creatures, as well as many kinds of coral. The reef is full of food and it's also a good place to hide from predators.

A **seahorse** is a fish, not a horse! It swims slowly with its body hanging straight down in the water. Its long snout is good for sucking up food.

Starfish don't swim. Instead, they walk! Underneath their star-shaped bodies are hundreds of little legs, like tiny tentacles. They use them to move slowly across the reef.

Coral is a colony of tiny animals called polyps. The polyps live in harmony with tiny plants called algae. In fact, some of the beautiful colors of coral are created by this algae.

The coral reef is an ecosystem. This means that all of its plants and animals depend on each other. But the balance is delicate. Even a small rise in the temperature of the water can kill the coral. If the coral polyps die, the algae dies too, and the coral turns white. This is called bleaching.

The **clownfish** is immune to the sting of sea anemones, so it can hide among their tentacles for protection.

This huge creature is a humpback whale.
Be careful, little fish!
Don't get swallowed!

An adult humpback whale can weigh up to 60,000 lbs.
A whale calf weighs around 1,500 lbs.

Male **humpback whales** are famous for the songs they sing to attract female whales during mating season.

An American musician named David Rothenberg makes music with humpback whales! He goes out to sea in a small boat and drops a waterproof microphone and speaker into the water, so he can hear the whales and they can hear him. Then he listens to their song and plays the clarinet to accompany them.

You can find out more about his fascinating work on his website: *www.davidrothenberg.net*

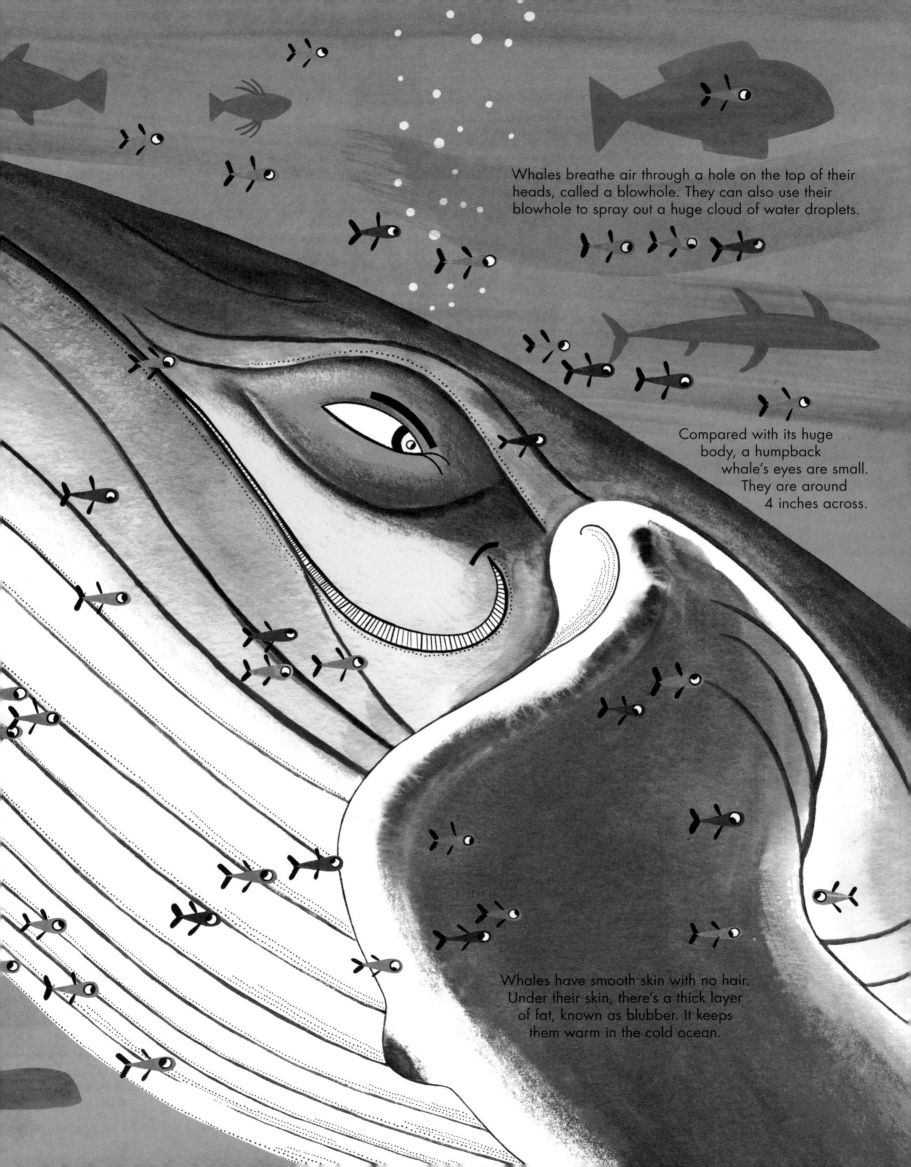

Whales breathe air through a hole on the top of their heads, called a blowhole. They can also use their blowhole to spray out a huge cloud of water droplets.

Compared with its huge body, a humpback whale's eyes are small. They are around 4 inches across.

Whales have smooth skin with no hair. Under their skin, there's a thick layer of fat, known as blubber. It keeps them warm in the cold ocean.

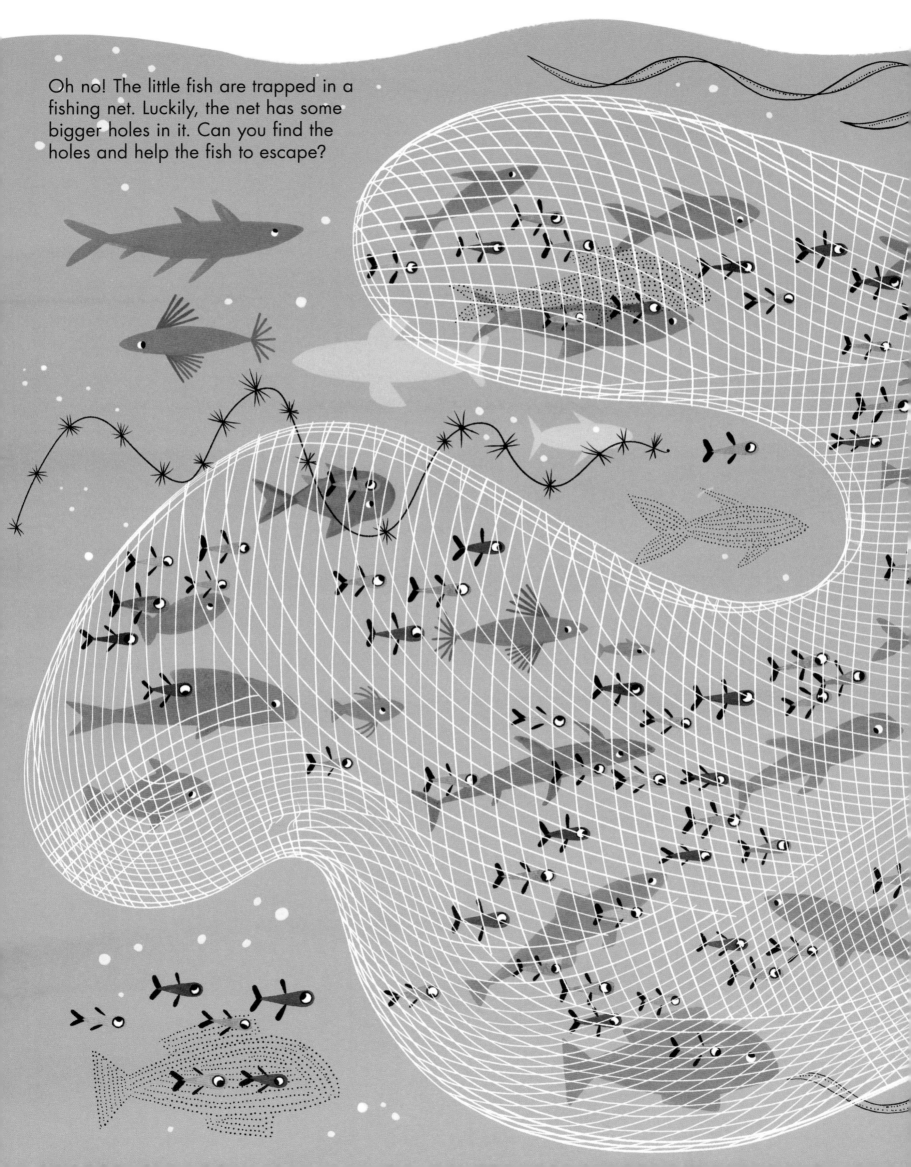

Oh no! The little fish are trapped in a fishing net. Luckily, the net has some bigger holes in it. Can you find the holes and help the fish to escape?

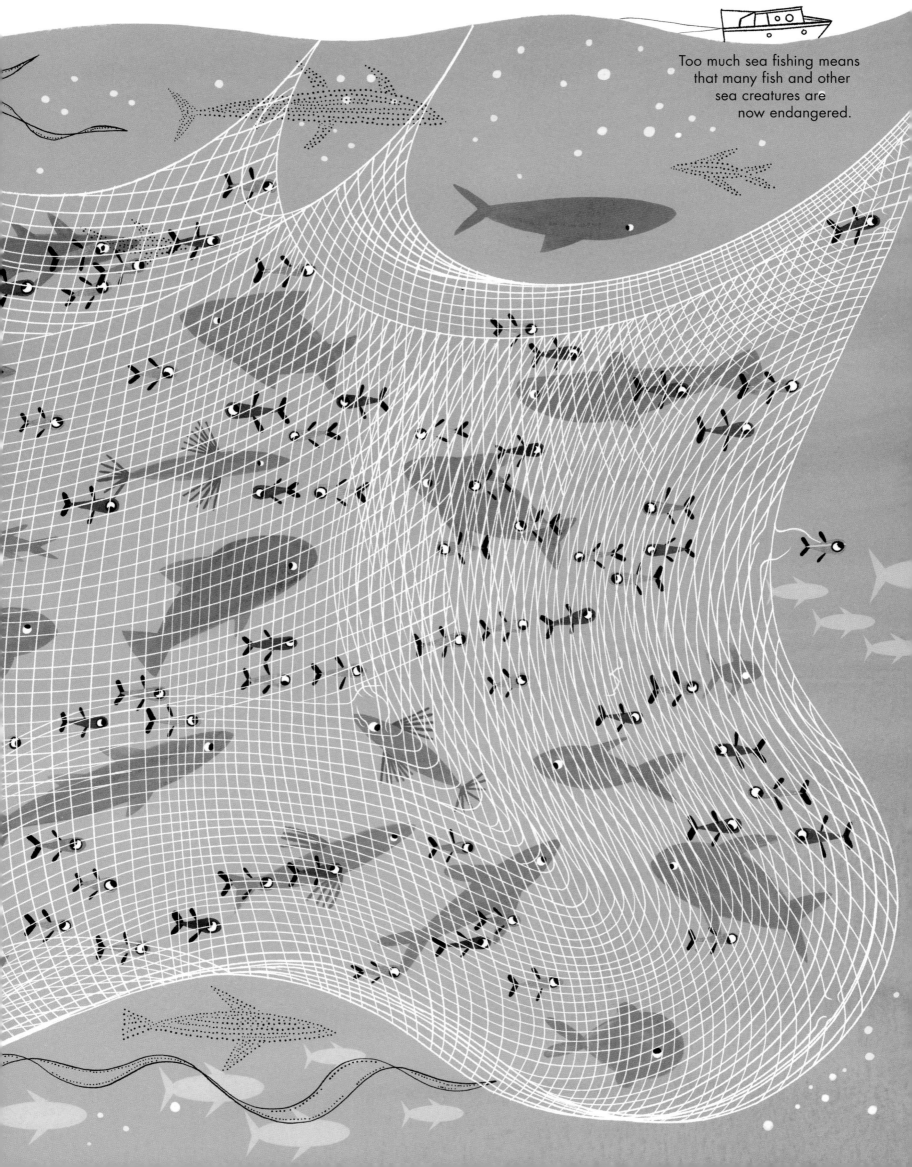

Too much sea fishing means that many fish and other sea creatures are now endangered.

Oh dear, these things aren't fish. How did all of this garbage end up in the ocean?
This is why we should try to buy fewer items made of plastic and recycle the plastic that we do buy.

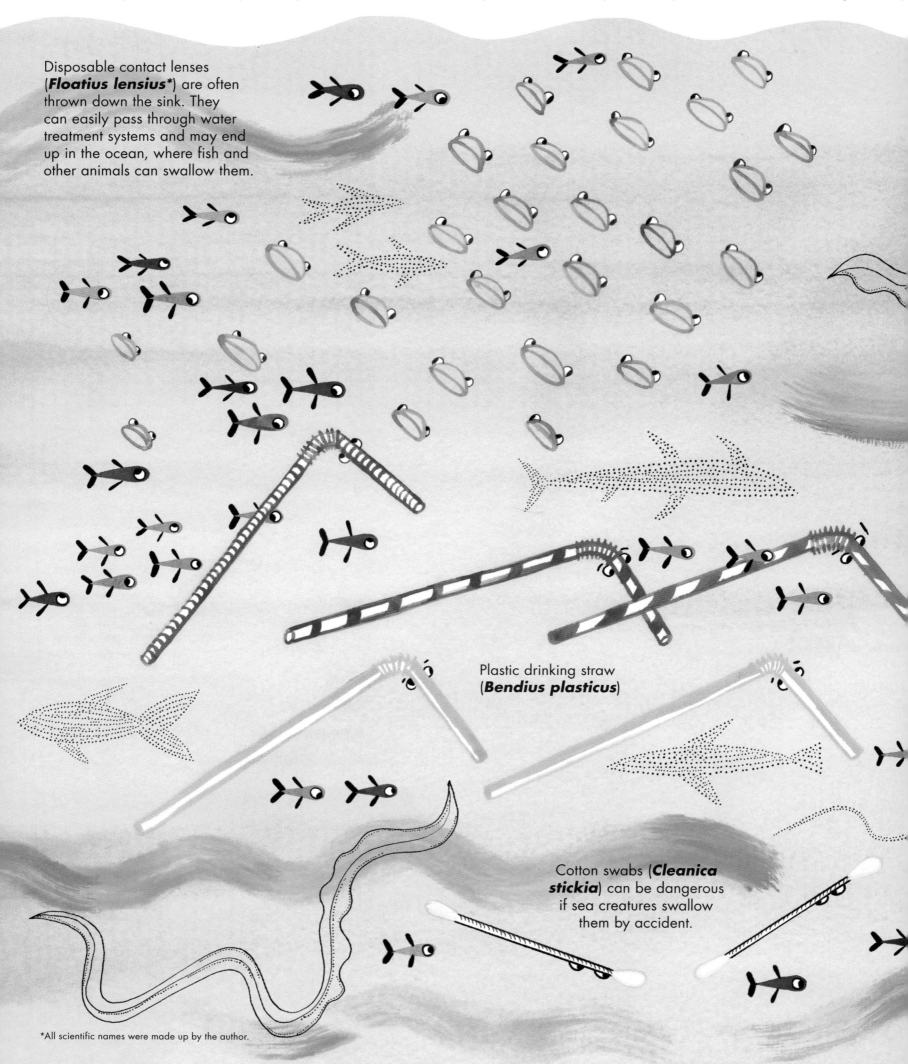

Disposable contact lenses (**Floatius lensius***) are often thrown down the sink. They can easily pass through water treatment systems and may end up in the ocean, where fish and other animals can swallow them.

Plastic drinking straw (**Bendius plasticus**)

Cotton swabs (**Cleanica stickia**) can be dangerous if sea creatures swallow them by accident.

*All scientific names were made up by the author.

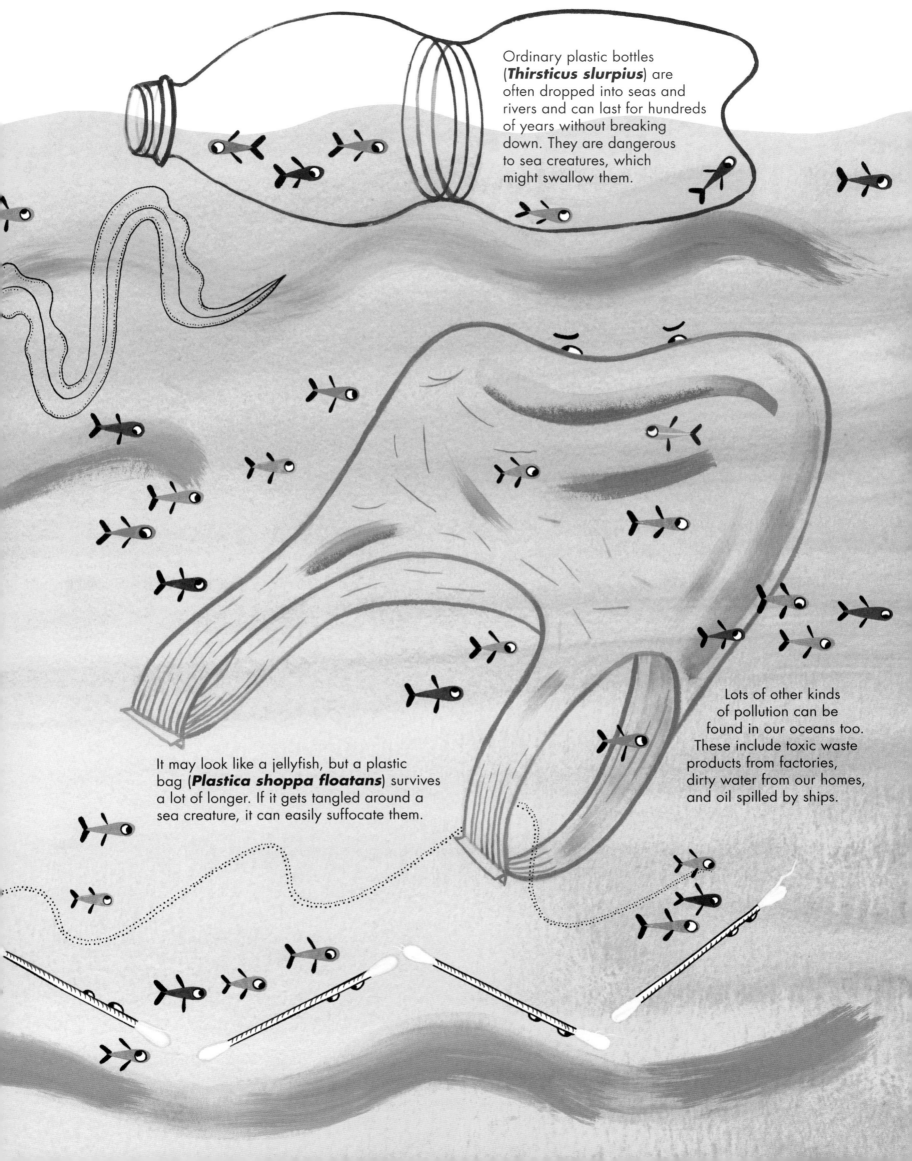

Ordinary plastic bottles (**Thirsticus slurpius**) are often dropped into seas and rivers and can last for hundreds of years without breaking down. They are dangerous to sea creatures, which might swallow them.

It may look like a jellyfish, but a plastic bag (**Plastica shoppa floatans**) survives a lot of longer. If it gets tangled around a sea creature, it can easily suffocate them.

Lots of other kinds of pollution can be found in our oceans too. These include toxic waste products from factories, dirty water from our homes, and oil spilled by ships.

Night is falling and it's getting dangerous to be out at sea. It's time to find a safe place to hide. Good luck, little fish!

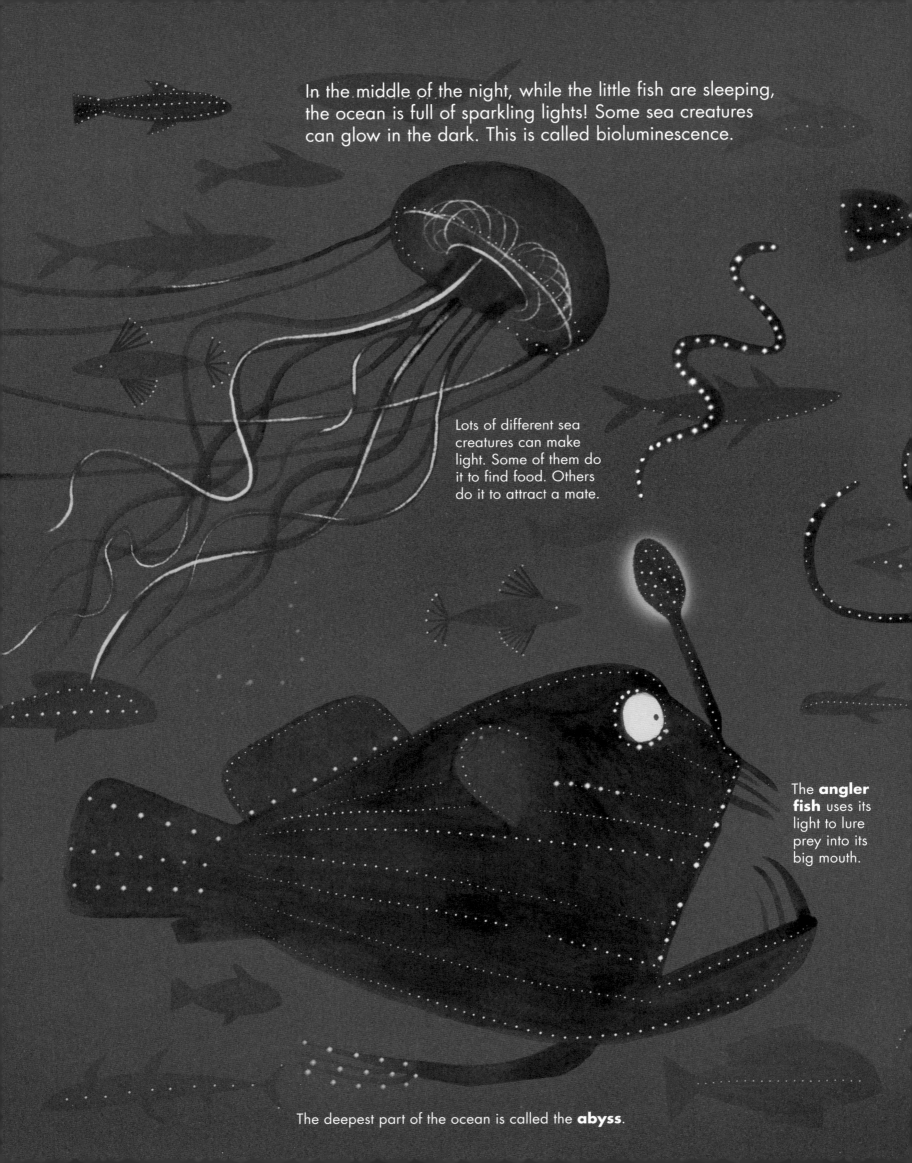

In the middle of the night, while the little fish are sleeping, the ocean is full of sparkling lights! Some sea creatures can glow in the dark. This is called bioluminescence.

Lots of different sea creatures can make light. Some of them do it to find food. Others do it to attract a mate.

The **angler fish** uses its light to lure prey into its big mouth.

The deepest part of the ocean is called the **abyss**.

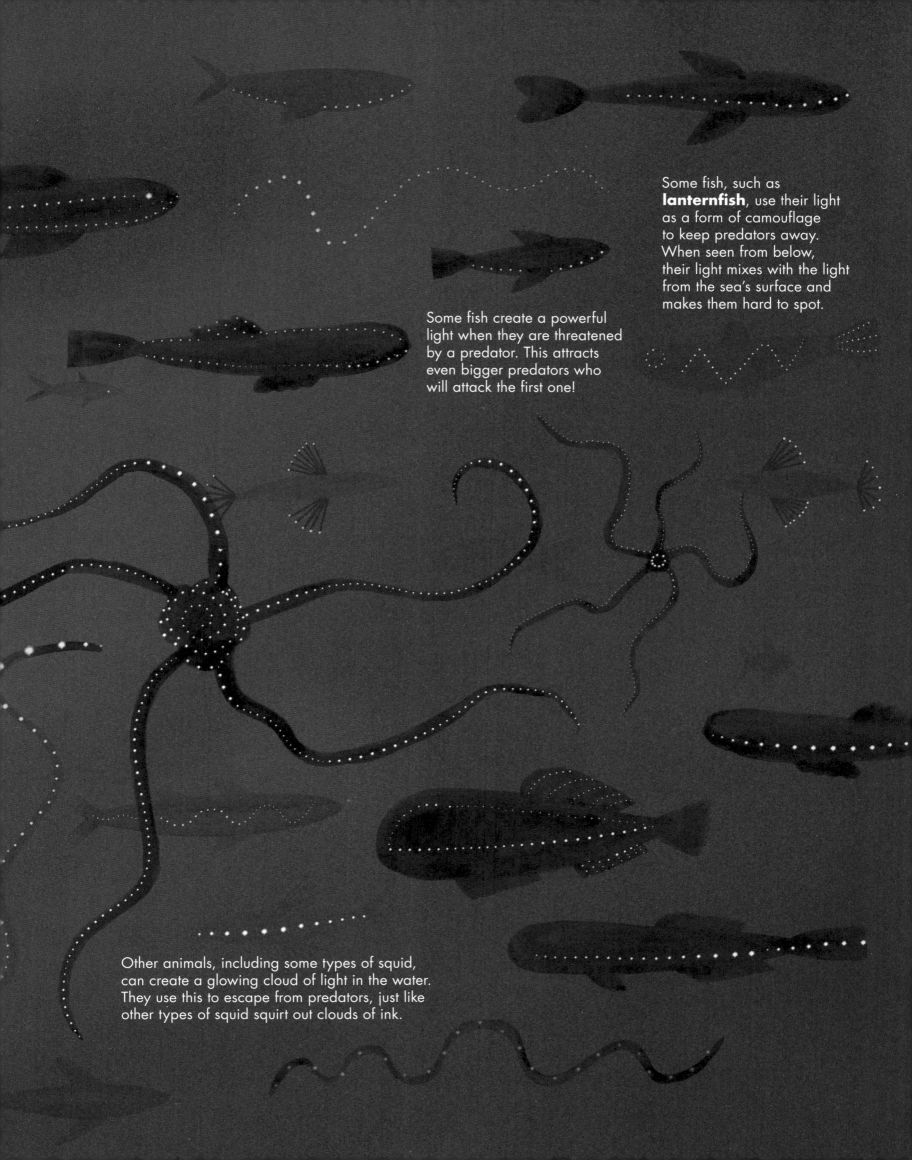

Some fish, such as **lanternfish**, use their light as a form of camouflage to keep predators away. When seen from below, their light mixes with the light from the sea's surface and makes them hard to spot.

Some fish create a powerful light when they are threatened by a predator. This attracts even bigger predators who will attack the first one!

Other animals, including some types of squid, can create a glowing cloud of light in the water. They use this to escape from predators, just like other types of squid squirt out clouds of ink.

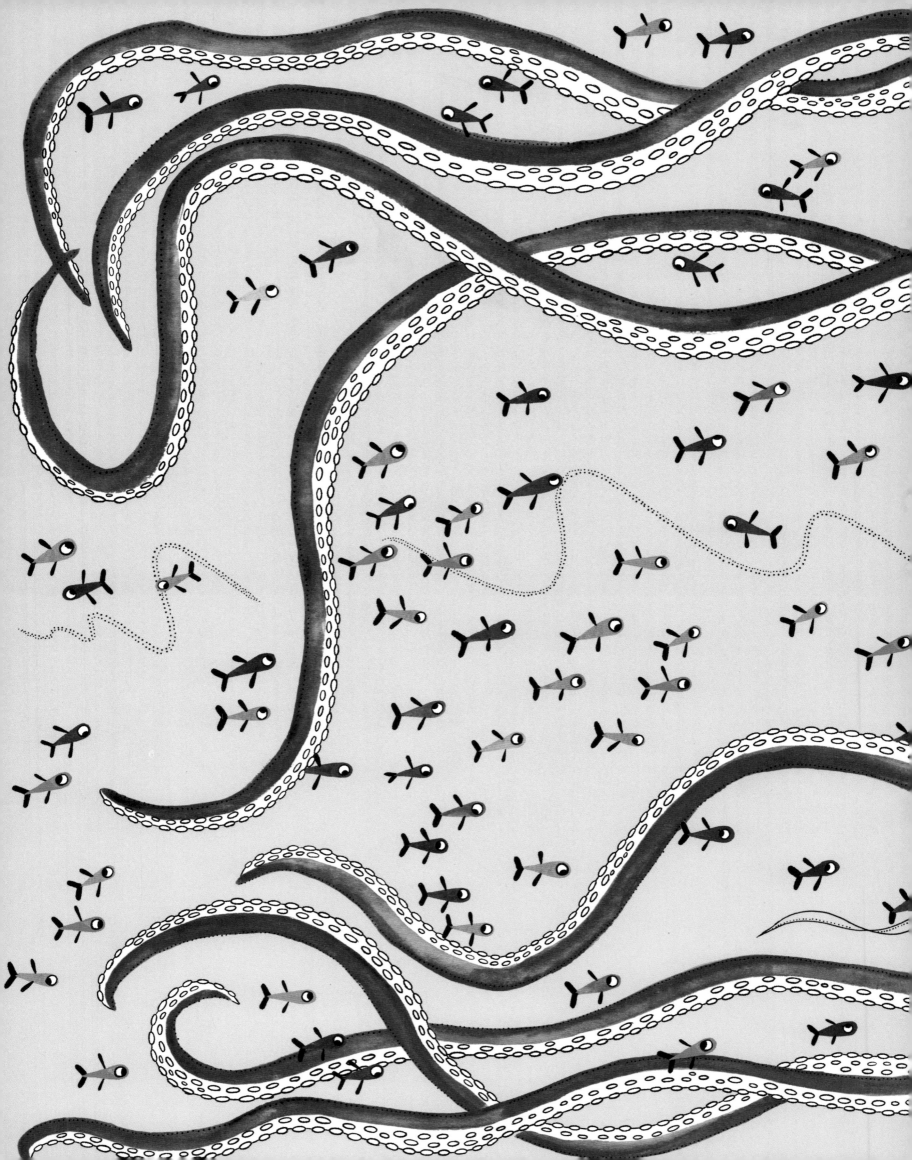